D0323644

Pass the Prosecco, Darling!

COOKING DISASTERS
AND OTHER KITCHEN DRAMAS

Liz Cowley

GIBSON SQUARE

For Cyd Barker
– great friend and cook, and the muse for this book

Also by Liz Cowley

Outside in My Dressing Gown
Gardening in Slippers
We All Have Our Moments
Serial Damage

This edition published for the first time by Gibson Square

UK   Tel: +44 (0)20 7096 1100
US   Tel: +1 646 216 9813

    rights@gibsonsquare.com
    www.gibsonsquare.com

    ISBN   9781783341344

The moral right of Liz Cowley to be identified as the author of this work has been asserted in accordance with the Copyright, Designs and Patents Act 1988.

All rights reserved. No part of this publication may be reproduced, stored in a retrieval system, or transmitted, in any form or by any means, electronic, mechanical, photocopying, recording or otherwise without the prior consent of the publisher. A catalogue record for this book is available from the Library of Congress and the British Library. © by Liz Cowley.

Cover illustration by Dorrance.

Papers used by Gibson Square are natural, recyclable products made from wood grown in sustainable forests; inks used are vegetable based. Manufacturing conforms to ISO 14001, and is accredited to FSC and PEFC chain of custody schemes. Colour-printing is through a certified CarbonNeutral® company that offsets its CO2 emissions.

Printed by CPI.

CONTENTS

GOOD FRIENDS ROUND THE TABLE

TAKE A WOMAN AND A MAN

BAKE-OFF

POST MORTEMS

'Pass the Prosecco, Darling!'

'PASS THE PROSECCO, DARLING!'

'Any more Prosecco, darling?
And have you thought of what to cook?'
'No, but see the files behind me?
I find they're always worth a look'……

'TOO DIFFICULT.' 'NO-ONE ATE IT.'
'TOO TIME-CONSUMING.' 'TURNED OUT CRAP.'
'LOOKED NOTHING LIKE THE PHOTO DID –
THE ONE ON THE FRONT COVER FLAP.'

'TOO EXPENSIVE.' 'FAR TOO FIDDLY.'
'A WASTE OF TIME – IT TOOK ALL DAY.'
'NO-ONE HAD A SECOND HELPING.'
'I ENDED THROWING HALF AWAY.'

'SOUPS AND STEWS THAT AREN'T GOOD NEWS
AND TURNED INTO A LOAD OF SLOSH.'
'MORE DINNER DISHES NOT TO DO
THAT FRANKLY JUST AREN'T WORTH THE DOSH.'

Recording rotten recipes –
what great advice for hostesses!

THE PHONE

'Don't forget, James can't stand beetroot,
and as you know, I'm dieting!
So don't make any pud for me.
And can we bring you anything?'

'Hi, is that Liz? I thought I'd ring.
We're looking forward to tonight,
unless it's curry! Don't forget!
Well, knowing you, we thought you might!'

'Hi, just checking when you want us.
And Liz, I have one small request.
John's been told to cut out salt.
He failed the latest doctor's test.

Could you put it on the table
but not in any pot or pan?
Hoping that you get this message.
I'd be so grateful if you can!'

'Hi, Liz, thought I'd better call you.
I hope you don't think this is rude,
but now we're going low on carbs
please count us out of starchy food.'

'Hi, darling! See you both at eight,
but Jim won't eat much, I'm afraid.
He's had a massive business lunch
at which he rather overstayed.

You know those director lunches!
So, not too much upon his plate.
Oh, one more thing, he's now asleep.
We may be there a wee bit late!'

Not unusual, phone calls like that,
and often on the very day.
Next time I ask them (if I do!),
I'll buy them all a takeaway.

'OUCH!'

The doorbell rings. 'Hi! Great to see you!'
Have we invited them to stay?
They've got two cases at their feet.
We can't ask them to go away.

What's in the freezer or the fridge?
Well, nothing I can cook tonight.
What's more we're off to France at dawn
to catch the early morning flight.

And who'll admit we're off in hours?
My goodness, that will take some tact.
And even worse, we'll have to say
that neither one of us has packed.

The fridge is empty, ditto freezer.
A dinner out it has to be.
Who'd forgotten they were coming?
My husband? No, me, probably!

HALFWAY THROUGH YOUR OWN DINNER PARTY

Oh my God, I've just remembered!
We should have gone to Anne and Nick.

Today's the eighteenth, isn't it?
Now what to do? I feel quite sick.

How awful, but what can we do?
They're sure to call us in a mo.

(They do, of course. We tell our guests
that they can stay, but we must go.)

DOROTHY AT THE DOOR

'Dorothy, you look fantastic!
Where are you off to? Somewhere smart?'
'Well, you asked me round to dinner.'
Gosh, did I? Not the greatest start.

And nor, alas, was what came after –
the England final on TV.
My husband said he had to watch,
so I did too, and Dorothy.

TV trays don't go with diamonds,
nor dog hairs with a Prada dress.
Poor Dorothy, and also me.
An evening of sheer hellishness.

Eat with her, and in the kitchen?
No, terribly embarrassing.
Anyway, the fridge was empty,
devoid of almost anything.

When England won, my husband whooped,
but not so me and Dorothy.
The dog, alarmed, knocked off her tray,
and sadly, somewhat messily.

Forgiveness is a marvellous thing,
but never came from Dorothy.
And now we've not seen her in years,
perhaps not that surprisingly.

DOUBLE BOOKING

'Why, darling, are we driving North?'
'To dine with Mike and Marianne.'
'Oh God, I think we've double-booked.
I said we'd go to Jill and Stan.'

The car skids to a sudden halt.
Now, who'd be least pissed off with us?
Well, Marianne, quite probably.
Less likely she would make a fuss.

Embarrassed, I call Marianne.
'Thank God!' she said. 'We've just caught flu.
In fact, we've both been panicking.
For ages we've been calling *you*!'

Oh what a blessing, mobile phones,
though endless texts can be a bore.
That night, it truly dawned on us
just what a mobile phone is for.

GOOD LORD

What's she wearing? Golly, quite fantastic!
But diamonds for a simple supper here?
Did I say 'smart'? No, of course I didn't!
Now, in my jeans, I want to disappear.

A Gucci suit, that necklace and Louboutins?
Well, even at a grand do, OTT.
Should have got to know her rather better,
before extending hospitality!

I should be more careful asking strangers.
What did I say? I truly can't be sure.
And I'm not the only one embarrassed,
while staring at each other at the door.

'Have I got the wrong night?' She looks worried.
'No, do come in!' I smile. What else to do?
Can't leave her both hungry and embarrassed.
Quite probably it's happened to you too.

A FRIEND TO STAY

Ever had a friend to stay
who doesn't do things quite your way –
like tossing round the cutlery
so all of it sits crookedly,
or oiling spuds you want to bake
(which end up soft, for heaven's sake),
and never washes lettuces
(though told just where the whizzer is),
and even makes a hash of mash
by mashing it in such a flash
it ends up full of lumps and bumps?
My goodness, I can get the grumps.
I tell myself that help is nice
and do not proffer my advice.
But it can be so frustrating,
and at times, most irritating!

WHAT THE HELL TO COOK?

Now, how about a main of fish
and that great sauce I did with lime?
Oh, blast, I'm sure that was the dish
I gave to John and Sue last time.

A boeuf en croûte? I do that well,
it's always something of a treat.
Oh, damn and blast and bloody hell,
Suzanne and Philip don't eat meat.

Paella? That might fit the bill –
I got quite good at that in Spain.
No, hang on, prawns make Anna ill.
I can't make that mistake again.

I know, I'll do a salmon trout.
Oh, no! Diana always moans
unless the backbone's taken out
and all those fiddly little bones.

Or why not take the whole lot out?
No, that idea is truly daft.
The meal will have to be my shout,
and that won't help my overdraft.

Oh, damn and hell, two days to go,
and still I'm stuck for what to do.
There must be something. Ah, I know,
I'll ring and say I've just caught flu!

'FORGETFULNESS IS A FORM OF FREEDOM.'

Kahlil Gibran

'Liz, aren't you coming in to do the lunch?'
My husband calls me from the kitchen door.
Help! I'd quite forgotten asking friends round
while busy planting out four hours or more.

Eight for lunch; no time to do the shopping.
Now what to do? They're here in half an hour.
Order several pizzas? I'd feel guilty.
Not even time to have a decent shower.

What's the time? Good God, I can't believe it!
I must have been outside since ten to eight.
Tell my friends the lunch has just been cancelled?
Oh God, I can't do that; it's far too late.

Time outside can make me absent-minded,
beguiled, besotted, in a total trance,
quite forgetting people I've invited
while choosing pleasant places for my plants.

Planting out soon puts me in a dream world;
all part, I think, of what a garden's for.
Then the dream world turns into a nightmare
when friends arrive too early at the door.

Ouch! They're here, while I'm still in the bathroom!
There's nothing I can do but go on down.
Where's my husband? Gone to do the shopping.
What's more, it's now mud brown, my dressing gown.

BREAKFAST

Breakfast – not my favourite time.
It's when I like my private space.
But when I have my mates to stay,
I force a smile upon my face.

My head is with the fairies then
and clatter can make me irate.
'Liz, do you have some marmalade?
And can I have a bigger plate?

And where's it kept, the frying pan?
I fetch it, somewhat grumpily,
but hide my mood as best I can.
Those chatty breakfasts – not for me.

Breakfast – not a meal I relish,
preferring silences first thing,
I don't like people chattering
and cutlery all clattering.

I wish I was a 'first thing' person.
In fact, I am – in my own space.
I'll just have to get used to it
and show a little bit more grace.

YOUR PRECIOUS DAMASK CLOTH

If someone knocked the red wine over
and on your precious damask cloth,
turning it from white to scarlet,
would you stay calm or show your wrath?

Would you jump up and clear the table
and rush the cloth off for a soak,
or sprinkle salt upon the stain,
although, inside, you want to choke?

What would I do? I'm not quite sure,
but think I'd sprinkle it with salt,
and then (because I'm far too wet)
I'd hear my voice say 'Not your fault!'

A FAVOURITE MUG

Like me, a friend has loads of mugs,
but only uses one herself.
And how she hates it if you pick
that favourite mug from off her shelf!
'I'm sorry, darling, that's *my* mug.
Please, can you pick another one?'
At last, I've learned that, in her house,
to choose that mug just can't be done.
I guess we all have funny ways
and quirky eccentricities.
And now I *never* touch that mug.
I know exactly whose it is!

THE FLOWER ARRANGEMENT

A lovely floral centrepiece.
But now I can't see anyone –
at least, the people opposite.
This dinner won't be that much fun.

A nice arrangement – beautiful.
But now I'm stuck for several hours
trying to speak to other guests
blocked off behind those bloody flowers.

Can I ask her to remove them?
No, she might think that's impolite.
What a bore to peer around them!
It won't be that much fun tonight.

It's sometimes best to lower goals,
with flowers, as it is with food.
And stand up when you wish to speak?
You can't – that would be far too rude.

THANK YOU, BUT NO THANK YOU!

Thank you, but no thank you. Someone's cleared up.
And now I just can't find a bloody thing.
Where's she put the plates, the bowls, the glasses?
I wish she'd gone to bed, left everything!

Thank you, but no thank you for your help here.
It's kind of you to clear up after me.
But, alas, it's also irritating
when nothing's back where it's supposed to be.

When I told you 'Leave it', well, I meant it,
and thought, like me, you'd soon be up in bed.
Now I'll spend all morning sorting out things.
I wish you'd left a mess down here instead.

Guests who clear up – full of good intentions.
I smile and thank them when they've come on down.
Little do they know I'm irritated,
but much too kind to do as much as frown.

MUFFIN

Wherever is the birthday cake?
Inside the dog – and every crumb,
and all ten candles that were there.
What agony in Muffin's tum!

I rush him to the local vet.
The operation costs a mint.
And so did all those goodie bags,
so now I'm feeling doubly skint.

The party – also a dog's dinner
without me there to organise.
The dog survived, I'm glad to say.
At least that was a nice surprise.

STROGANOFF

'Mmm! What's that? It smells delicious.'
A great aroma fills the air.
I recognise it – Stroganoff.
How lucky to be lunching there!

A hound bounds in and sniffs around.
He also loves that smell, like me.
'Nearly ready!' says my friend.
The dog jumps up excitedly.

It's huge, a Bernese mountain dog –
a massive breed with loads of fur.
My goodness, she might drop the pot –
his paws are now all over her!

'Down Bilko, down, you naughty boy!
This pot is hot, and heavy too.
Down boy, or you'll send me flying
and pouring food all over you!'

My God, she's filling up his bowl!
'His favourite meal!' I hear her say.
And what do we eat? *Sandwiches.*
I never will forget that day!

FOOD FOR THOUGHT

Food, I think, is taking over
and making many people mad,
obsessing them with what is healthy
and what is not. I find that sad.
And what will age us, give us wrinkles,
or cut our life expectancy.
It's why I wrote this little book.
Cuisine's so often comedy.

RECIPES FOR IRRITATION

Why *does* it have to be Thai basil?
Why *does* it have to be Welsh lamb?
Will anybody even notice?
Will anybody give a damn?
Like almost everyone who cooks,
I'm all for a good recipe,
but chefs, why make them such hard work,
and harder than they need to be?
Why *does* it matter where things come from?
And will the difference really show?
Perhaps, if you're a gourmet chef,
but surely no-one else will know.

UNUSED RECIPES

How many dishes have you done
from all the many books you own?
Loads from this one, none from that one?
Don't worry, you are not alone.

So few of us try everything.
In fact, that would be very rare.
Most recipes are wasted ones,
but count those up, we wouldn't dare.

It's scary checking out our books.
Well-thumbed pages? Not that many.
And whole books that we've never used?
Even they are two a penny.

No point though in feeling guilty.
Try checking out a good friend's books.
Loads of pristine, unused pages,
in common with most other cooks!

'I'M SURE THIS WILL BE A FLOP.'

One ingredient that's missing –
so very often – confidence.
The pressure from those TV shows
to cook great food is so immense.

Just keep it simple, that's my rule.
We can't all cook like Michel Roux.
Turn off the telly, my advice,
and simply stop attempting to!

THE LONG AND THE SHORT OF IT

The longer is the recipe,
the less it will appeal to me.
The more chance I'll get something wrong
if recipes go on too long.

Thank God most chefs have reached the stage
their recipes fit just one page,
or even better, just one half
complete with a nice photograph.

No photos? You can count me out,
and many other cooks, no doubt.
A wodge of type has no appeal.
We need a picture of the meal.

However, chefs, a simple tip
on where you sometimes tend to slip.
Don't photograph the scenery
in France or Greece or Italy.

We want to see the finished dish,
not where it comes from, meat or fish.
Forget about the fields and seas
and sheep in pretty meadows, please!

And though a market's nice to see,
we want good *food* photography.
Those 'atmos' shots make pretty books,
but ones that aren't much help to cooks.

Show rustic kitchens, by all means,
and charming little farmhouse scenes,
as long as we can also see
what helps us with the cookery!

'EAT SOMETHING UNCOOKED ONCE A DAY.'

Professor Arthur de Vaney, in his book 'The New Evolution Diet'.

Thanks for that advice, dear Arthur.
That helps a lazy type like me.
With one less meal to cook each day,
that suits my lifestyle splendidly.
Great excuse for much less cooking –
that's why I so enjoyed your book.
Cooked lunch now is off the menu.
And once a day, I'm of the hook.
(Of course, I've taken your advice
a wee bit further than you meant,
but all the same, I love you for it.
In fact, your book is heaven sent.)

A PAPERLESS KITCHEN

I'm always snipping recipes from papers
and putting them in files to do one day.
But that day never comes, so I unclick them
and throw another pile of them away.

I'm always such a sucker for new dishes
(and mostly ones that I will never do)
crammed in files and making me feel guilty
and taking too much kitchen space up too.

Procrastination – death of new ideas,
and all those files make kitchens such a mess.
A better bet – to check the internet,
and have a kitchen almost paperless.

TOO MANY BOOKS GATHER THE DUST

Fifty, sixty, maybe eighty cook books,
but which are used? If you're at all like me,
dozens of them sit there, barely opened.
And still, it grows, my kitchen library.

Most too complex, marvellous to look at.
But who wants recipes that last all day?
But they look so lovely, all those cookbooks,
I just can't bear to chuck a load away.

They're piled behind a row of coffee mugs.
They're just the same, we need no more than eight.
Hoarder – that is me, and not a thrower,
and chucking out nice things I truly hate.

I'll have to face the fact that I'm a junkie,
and also that I'm not about to change.
And luckily, in other people's kitchens,
I often notice hoarding isn't strange.

MY HEROINE

Elizabeth David, great chef and writer –
the best of all cooks and chefs that I know.
But oh, what a shame you didn't have photos.
That would have helped your legend to grow!
Pictures are edible, often so beautiful.
How could you publish without just one shot?
It's cheaper to buy you, and cheaper to try you,
though a great picture can help such a lot!

PRE-DINNER DRINKS

My friends are always telling me
our kitchen's like a library.
It is. It's stuffed with loads of books
(besides the ones on cookery).

My husband loves all books on war,
he's mad about the military.
You want to put your wine glass down?
The floor's the only space that's free.

I'm just as bad at collecting books
on gardening, and poetry.
You want to rest your glass awhile?
Once more, the floor it has to be.

There's nowhere to put down your glass.
There's simply not one space that's free.
Well, only on the top of books
which people don't do normally.

The answer – just hang on to it,
or else just put it by your feet
until I've got the dinner done
and tell you all it's time to eat.

Oh, the smashing times we've had here
with glasses left upon the floor!
But never mind, they're all from Poundland.
A pound – that's all it costs for four.

AT THE FARMER'S MARKET

Mud, mud, glorious mud –
nothing quite like it when buying a spud.
I know that sounds quite manic,
but then spuds look organic.
I love a spud with bits of mud.
I think we all do, don't you?

Earth, earth, glorious earth
helps farmers sell spuds for more than they're worth.
You'll never find a bargain.
A higher price – a foregone.
But somehow mud is in our blood.
I think that's true, don't you?

From the rhythm of 'Mud, mud, glorious mud' by Flanders and Swann

A RUSTIC BASKET

Funny how a rustic basket
can make a shopping trip more fun.
Oh, so much nicer than a bag,
especially a plastic one.

Funny how a rustic basket
(especially one that's made of straw)
can put a spring within your step
when going out of your front door.

All those times I go out shopping
can sometimes make my spirits sag,
but not when I'm a basket case
and go without a plastic bag.

'MMM!'

'Mmm, that's such a lovely perfume!'
(My butcher – such a flatterer!)
'It's Opium, if I'm not wrong.'
It is, I readily concur.

And then, instead of sausages,
I buy two steaks, despite the price,
as probably he guessed I would.
Still, flattery is always nice.
What butcher's ever said to you
he loves your perfume? Surely rare.
A rather clever ruse, I think,
to make me buy the best things there!

THE SUNDAYS

Looking through the pages of the Sundays,
I find what looks a smashing recipe.
But two things needed I have never heard of.
And will I find them? No, not easily.

Boring – searching round the supermarket
for things I maybe wouldn't recognise.
And would staff know them? Possibly unlikely.
If not, that wouldn't come as a surprise.

Something I don't know can put me off things,
and finding where it is can be a bore.
Cookery, ideally should be stress-free.
It's not, if you can't find things in a store.

SUPERMARKETS

Oh blast, they've changed things round again!
I wish they'd leave things where they were.
A layout that stays much the same
is surely one we'd all prefer.
We know exactly where things are,
then suddenly the layout's new,
and now, instead of half an hour,
our shopping takes an age to do.
The veg has moved, and so has meat,
and where on earth to find the bread?
It's now a maze, no fun at all
to try and get the family fed.
We ask assistants where things are;
they're always at the other end.
Of course, Sod's Law, and such a bore –
it always drives me round the bend.
Please, supermarkets – think of us!
And don't keep changing layouts round,
so shopping isn't such a stress
and certain foods are never found!

LOVE IT OR LOATHE IT

Some food is like that.
Love it, or loathe it.
Beetroot is like that.
A taste that some hate.
Best to put some things
in separate dishes.
Risky to put them
on somebody's plate.

Curry is like that,
garlic is like that,
grapefruit is like that.
Well, some things just are.
Love it, or loathe it.
Most of all, Marmite.
It's gathering dust,
my ten year old jar.

TABLE NAPKINS

Table napkins, now redundant.
Guests rarely use them any more.
Mostly left beside the plate
or found next morning on the floor.
Why bother putting napkins out?
One more thing I don't need to do.
Why *do* I go the extra mile,
and even when it's me and you?
Another thing to wash and iron
or put back in the kitchen drawer.
Why *do* we bother with all that?
Why give ourselves another chore?

MISMATCH

Our cupboards – full of dinner plates.
Some gorgeous – but there's one big catch.
We've had them all for years and years,
and now no more than four will match.

Most folk would chuck the whole lot out,
but what a waste, and what a shame
when tables can look prettier
with no two dinner plates the same.

A DINING ROOM? NO, SCARY!

I'm glad that we don't have a dining room,
especially one that's ultra chic and sleek.
Rooms like that would raise guests' expectations
and planning what to cook would take a week.
Cosy family kitchens – so much better,
in fact, I think the greatest recipe
for entertaining in an atmosphere
of happiness and informality.

Each time we eat in someone's dining room,
I somehow think the food will be a hit.
Expectations always soar much higher,
the smarter is the place in which we sit.
Cosy settings lower expectations.
If things aren't perfect, then it matters less.
Old-fashioned kitchens – perfect recipe
for entertaining friends with far less stress!

A GREAT DIVERSION

Scatter blossoms down the table.
If what you cook is not a hit,
the chances are that not one guest
will look back and remember it.

Great attention-getters – blossoms –
if dishes don't turn out quite right.
Guests won't remember your mistakes
when tables look a sheer delight.

When attempting brand new dishes,
I often try the blossom ruse.
That will get the meal remembered
if what you serve is not great news.

'Gosh, Liz! Wow, the table's lovely!'
Those first impressions work a treat,
and even if the food you've done
was not, perhaps, your greatest feat!

A SWEET TOOTH

That's firmly missing in my mouth.
I've never had that sort of tooth,
but never say that to a host.
It's rather hard to tell the truth.

If they have made a smashing pud,
I think it's rather rude to say,
and even ruder it would be
to push the pudding dish away.

PLACE MATS

Mats – not needed at a table,
but put them out, I always do.
It's force of habit, I suppose,
but silly, when it's just us two.

It somehow looks more welcoming
to have a mat in front of you,
though cleaning mats up afterwards
is one more thing I needn't do.

Place mats mark out someone's space
and show a little bit of heart,
and pretty ones, with guests around,
are part of entertaining art.

And when it's only me at home,
mats make a meal out of a snack.
Forget a mat? I can't do that.
At my age there's no going back!

TALKING TO VEGETABLES

You come outside and talk to us –
you think that helps to make us grow.
You touch our leaves and say nice things
while walking up and down our row.

We grow for you, we put on weight –
your words are most encouraging,
and then when we are large and strong,
you do a most appalling thing.

You chop us down, you cut us up,
you boil us up and then you eat us,
and after all we've done for you.
How could you cheat and so mistreat us?

NO SUPERSTAR

One thing that I know I'll never be –
and that's a superstar at cookery,
although it never, ever worries me
that friends of mine might privately agree.
A good laugh round the table seems to me
to be the most successful recipe.
Far more important things in life than food,
and take the risk of boshing things – I would!

JUNK!

Kitchens – often more like junk shops
and crammed with things we never use –
things like fondue sets and raclettes
we once thought were terrific news.
Egg separators, sandwich-makers
and coffee frothers – who needs those?
And all those choppers and wine stoppers –
the list of rubbish grows and grows.
'Wine coolers' – crazy with a fridge
(or coolbag if we're in the car).
What's more, most coolers need a plug.
How crazy many gadgets are!
The latest fad – 'banana slicers'.
For God's sake, we can use a knife!
It very often seems to me
that more of us should get a life!

ONE INGREDIENT TO KEEP OUT

Stress – that's best kept off the menu,
but sadly it is often there –
hosts stressed out and panicking
and often tearing out their hair.

What the hell, if it's disastrous?
It's best to make a joke of it.
We're lucky to be asked at all,
and none of us will mind a bit.

If the soufflé hasn't risen,
and if the beef was overdone,
that won't matter if the chatter
turns out to be a lot of fun.

Who cares if it isn't perfect?
At least one thing will fetch some praise:
the very fact we've been asked out –
that's always pleasant nowadays.

SPAGHETTI

How to tell spaghetti's cooked?
Chuck a strand upon the wall.
If it's cooked, it stays stuck on,
but if it's not, then it will fall.

A somewhat unhygienic tip
that someone told me years ago,
but one that may well stain the wall
and with a mark that may not go!

BRUSSELS SPROUTS

I like my Brussels sprouts quite hard.
'Like bullets', says my great mate Trish.
I guess we all have different views
on how we like to do a dish.
I think a lot of vegetables
are far, far better underdone.
And if you don't like veg with crunch,
don't dine or lunch here, anyone!

PRAWNS

Left in the fridge a wee bit long.
Well, one day more than is ideal.
Throw them? Serve them – take the risk?
An awful shame to waste a meal.

Left one day late, what would you do?
I think I'd trust my sense of smell
(though many people never would).
I'd sniff and hope that all was well.

I think I'd tend to take the risk,
but saying that is dangerous.
It could mean someone reading this
would never come to dine with us!

LOBSTERS

Could I ever cook a lobster?
Alas, I couldn't. Far too kind.
The thought of boiling them alive?
Er, no, that truly blows my mind.

Even if they're pretty sleepy
(placed in the freezer for a bit)
I couldn't bring them to the boil.
I hate the very thought of it.

And, at restaurants serving lobster,
I don't like choosing them from tanks.
Choose my victim? I'd feel guilty.
It may be scrumptious, but no thanks!

COOKING WITH WINE

I always love to cook with wine,
and sometimes add it to the food.
I like to have a glass nearby.
Without one, my right hand feels nude.

I always love to cook with wine,
and now it is far too late to stop.
Who'd cook a meal for eight to ten
without imbibing just one drop.

EXTRA VIRGIN OLIVE OIL

How *do* we know it's 'extra virgin'?
Less virgin – could we really tell?
Just how good are people's taste-buds,
and come to that, our sense of smell?
As for all those different pressings,
will those who taste them ever know?
Maybe not in my opinion.
The difference doesn't really show.
(Of course it will, if you're a 'nose'
and working in the olive biz.)
But if a humble cook like me,
it's hard to spot the differences.
'Extra virgin' – is it worth it?
Yes, maybe to a well-trained 'nose'.
But why pay extra for an oil
if extra flavour hardly shows?

AGONY

Blast, I've forgotten to get the red wine.
The shops are all shut. And now what to do?
A bottle of Mouton Rothschild is there,
but oh, what a crime to chuck in a stew!

Ring round the neighbours? I haven't got time.
Make something else? No, the larder is bare.
Open the bottle? Nothing else for it.
I fetch the corkscrew in utter despair.

SOUPERFAST RECIPE FOR SIX

Slice six tomatoes, one per guest.
Chop basil leaves (and quite a few).
Chuck the whole lot in a blender.
Already you are halfway through.

Now add three pints of chicken stock,
and whirr round for a sec or two.
Then stir in crème fraiche, one full tub.
All finished, no more work to do!

Except to pour it in a bowl
and season it a little bit
and chill it well (about three hours).
Done! Simple! That's the end of it.

Why make life so complicated
and far more than it needs to be?
The trick is surely cutting work
and with a simple recipe!

'JUS'

'Jus' – that's a word I wish I'd never heard.
Is 'gravy' far too lowly for us now?
Why *does* the word 'jus' set my teeth on edge?
My God, that word can irritate – and how!

Does 'gravy' smack of Bisto for most chefs?
That could explain why menus call it *'jus'*.
But so pretentious does it always sound,
it always makes me flinch each time they do.

VICHYSSOISE

I've gone and wasted several hours
on making them 'soupe Vichyssoise'
which didn't work. It's in the sink –
now blocked. I pour a good stiff drink.

No starter then. A crisp or two
and carrot sticks will have to do.
And what's that horrid, acrid smell?
Oh, f..k! I've burned the duck as well!

And now the kitchen's full of smoke.
I take a breath and almost choke.
And even worse, the window's stuck.
I've finally run out of luck.

All cooks, I think, will know that night
when nothing ever turns out right.
What can we do? Pretend we're ill,
or face a whacking restaurant bill?

PARSLEY

Hurry up, parsley.
Please germinate.
Such a slow grower,
too long to wait.

Hurry up, parsley,
hurry up, seed.
Slow germinator,
last thing I need.

Bored of you, parsley,
checking your tray.
No bloody difference
day after day.

Patience – a virtue
you need with this plant.
Slow to get going,
and hurry, it can't.

Thanks a bunch, parsley,
for giving me none.
Such a slow grower –
you're never much fun!

DO YOU GROW CUCUMBERS AND MINT?

I served this soup to Albert Roux.
A terrifying thing to do.
He didn't have one bowl, but three!
I wallowed in the flattery.
Whose recipe? I wish I knew.
And so, I'm sure, would Albert Roux.
I know acknowledgements are due,
but don't know who to give them to.

Chilled Cucumber and Mint Soup – *serves 6*
2 cucumbers
1 bunch (about 12 stalks) mint
1 oz butter
1 small onion
¾ pint chicken stock
1 rounded tablespoon flour
½ pint milk
1 carton soured cream
salt and freshly milled pepper

Cut about two inches off one of the cucumbers and set aside for the garnish. Peel both
cucumbers, cut in half lengthways, remove seeds and cut the flesh coarsely.

Melt the butter in a saucepan. Peel and chop the onion, add to the pan and sauté gently until the
onion is soft but not brown. Add the cucumber and mint. Stir to mix, then add the chicken stock.
Bring to the boil and simmer for twenty minutes.

Blend the flour with the milk – stir or whisk, there should be no lumps. Add a little of the hot
chicken stock from the pan, blend well and then stir into the soup. Bring to the boil, simmer for
two to three minutes, then draw off the heat. Rub the soup through a sieve or purée in an electric
blender. Allow to cool. Add the soured cram and then chill well. Garnish with thin slices of
preserved cucumber and serve.

SEA TROUT

Catching a sea trout for dinner,
I couldn't cosh it on its head.
Alas, more kind that would have been
than waiting 'til the fish was dead.

My guilt stopped me from eating it.
I chucked it back into the sea.
Now, eating out and eating trout
brings back that guilty memory.

WILL THEY RISE?

Baking powder, so I'm told
can very quickly lose effect,
so cakes that you may want to bake
may not turn out as you expect.

It may not raise the sponge one inch.
In fact, your cakes may end up flat.
Perhaps you shouldn't take the risk,
unless you know you'll cope with that.

A wodge of cake can still taste nice,
and birds will love it, that's for sure.
And if the cake's as hard as nails,
then so are beaks outside the door!

RELAX, RELAX, RELAX, RELAXEZ-VOUS!

Everyone gets so stressed out now.
I think we should relax a bit.
If nothing turns out how it should,
they probably won't notice it.

Or if they do, they'll still be mates,
and if they aren't, what friends were they?
Even with disastrous food,
good friends will never stay away.

All those things on television
are making us neurotic souls.
Much better to cook simple things
and not have lofty cooking goals!

Good friends round a table

QUITE THE BEST RECIPE

Good friends sitting round the table –
a blessing often overlooked.
Always, always more important
than anything we may have cooked
(or anything we've overcooked
and even done disastrously).
Good mates there who'll all forgive you –
the most important recipe.

Everyone gets far too fazed now.
Who cares if dishes aren't a hit?
If nothing turns out how it should,
they probably won't notice it.
Or if they do, you'll still be mates,
and if you aren't, what friends were they?
Well, even with disastrous food
good mates will never stay away.

All those things on telly these days
are making us neurotic souls.
Much better to cook simple things
and greatly lower cooking goals.
Simplicity, best recipe.
And all of us should just relax,
and if our guests leave grumpily,
well, simply give those folk the axe!

WHO TO SIT WHERE?

Who to put by Marianne?
I don't think she could cope with Jim.
He'll only talk about himself.
What madness ever asking him!

And who to put by Alexandra?
Good listener it will have to be –
which counts out Bill and Philip too.
And I can't have her next to me.

And Florence can't sit next to Bob.
Her leftist views will drive him spare –
a long term Labour activist.
It's just not fair to put him there.

Why *did* we ask these people round?
And who to sit next door to whom?
They'll all be here in half an hour,
and still I can't sort out the room.

'It's payback time' I tell myself.
They've had us round. We owe them one.
But working out where they will sit
is quite the opposite of fun.

IRRITATING!

'Liz, only a weeny bit, please!
We went out to Buck's Club today.
After a lunch of three courses
I can't put that much food away.
No, that's too much! Just a spoonful –
I simply can't fit one more in.'

Why did I bother with dinner?
My patience, at times, can wear thin!

WHERE ON EARTH HAS WOODY GONE?

Where on earth has Woody gone?
I thought he'd gone up to the loo,
but find him on the spare room bed
and snoring rather loudly, too.
I leave him be and go downstairs.
He clearly needs a bit of rest.
But what a funny thing to do,
invited as a dinner guest!
I tell myself he needs a kip,
and also that it's getting late.
At least he hasn't nodded off
and crashed into his pudding plate.
Entertaining 'til the small hours
I guess we've all seen sleepyheads
struggling to keep up with things
while quietly longing for their beds.

DOERS AND LEAVERS

A doer or a leaver?
Which of them are you?
You're one of them, that's certain.
It's almost always true.

Well, do you wash up last thing
and leave a spotless sink?
Some people simply have to,
or else can't sleep a wink

Others can't be bothered,
they never touch a thing.
They leave it all 'til morning
and then do everything.

Lots of folk would loathe that –
to come down to a mess.
They have to leave things tidy.
Not me, I must confess.

Out there are two big armies
who very often fight –
the doers versus leavers
who won't wash up at night.

I rarely enter battle
'til people come and stay,
and always it's the doers
who seem to win the day.

Best to let them do it,
and wander off to bed.
After all, who was it
who made sure they were fed?

THE DEMON DRINK

Jim's had one too many, and Larry more like four.
Worse, his golf-club stories have now become a bore.
Betty's now embarrassed about her husband Jim,
doing her best, poor woman, to try and silence him.
Usually a fun man, a most amusing bloke,
now he can't remember the punchline of a joke.
Not the greatest evening – but what is one to do?
Bite your lip, get through it. I guess it's nothing new!

PLEASE DON'T STAB YOUR KNIFE AT ME!

Please don't stab your knife at me
to reinforce your point of view.
For God's sake, put it down at once!
What if I pointed mine at you?

And do you have to wear your napkin
stuffed in your collar quite like that?
It makes you look, well, so old-fashioned,
and frankly, darling, such a prat!

And please, above all, don't come early,
or turn up here bang on the dot.
(All things of course I never say,
although I'd like to quite a lot!)

ANNOYING HABITS

People peeking in your pans
to see what you are cooking there –
that's a most annoying habit,
and one I truly cannot bear.

People tasting things in pans?
Now that is *seriously* rude,
specially if they use their fingers
to take a dollop of the food.

And loading up the dishwasher
between each course – that drives me mad.
It takes away the atmosphere
and ruined parties that I've had.

I want the plates left by the sink,
and ditto all the cutlery,
and don't want people jumping up
and promptly crashing into me.

Their help is nice, but not right then,
and never welcome late at night.
I want things left just where they are,
so I can clear up at first light.

Am I the only one who's miffed
by people wanting to assist,
and making all that clattering
and dropping things if they are pissed?

The one time that I like some help
is when we're running out of booze.
Please fetch a bottle, by all means.
The only time that help's good news!

DON'T ADD SALT UNTIL YOU'VE TASTED IT!

One of my few irritations –
guests far too ready with the salt
before they've even tasted things.
It's now too salty? Well, their fault!

Picking up the salt and pepper
before they've lifted cutlery
can irritate me quite a bit.
I sit there, fuming silently.

It's usually blokes from public schools
who camouflaged their tasteless food,
and should be told by somebody
that salting food like that is rude.

Why the hell has no-one told them?
Alas, it's not for me to do.
Instead, I sit and bite my lip,
although I'm sorely tempted to!

SLOW EATERS, FAST EATERS

Slow eater, me. Fast eater, you.
You've finished now, I'm halfway through.
Hosts often think if you are slow
(I found this out some years ago)
if slow, you don't much like the food.
Must hurry up – too slow looks rude!

'A DINNER PARTY'

These days, the phrase 'a dinner party'
is not one that I ever use.
Best to say 'a supper party'
in case the food is not great news.

Make a bosh, and 'dinner party'
sounds far too posh and OTT.
Safer to say 'supper party'
in case things go disastrously.

The more informal mealtimes sound
the more guests will forgive the host
if things don't turn out all that well,
or if you've overcooked the roast.

These days, I don't say 'dinner party.'
To me, that is a dangerous phrase.
The trick today – not sounding smart.
That's far, far safer nowadays.

Or simply use the one word, 'dinner',
and then ignore the 'party' bit.
That helps if nothing turns out right,
and guests are leaving half of it.

RESTING ARMS UPON THE TABLE

Arms and elbows on the table
used not to be considered polite –
at least in England, though abroad
the custom was thought quite alright.
And why? The English, I've been told
were always trusted not to steal
(from underneath the table height)
their neighbour's pockets at the meal.

FOOD SNOB

Why *do* some people hold knives like a pen?
Far harder to cut what's there on the plate.
Perhaps it's because their parents did that,
and now they can't change, it's simply too late.
Why wield a knife that can't exert pressure,
specially when cutting a chop or a steak?
Why make a knife a problem in life?
Hold the thing properly, for heaven's sake!
When held like a pen, it simply can't slice,
and held in that way it can't do its job.
And yes, I admit this very last bit –
with knives held that way, I can be a snob!

ANATHEMA!

Guests peeking at their mobile phones
(and underneath the table height)
should know the chance is pretty slim
that they'll be asked another night.

Why can't you wait until you've gone
to pick up all your messages?
Doing that at dinner parties?
Oh, how discourteous that is!

You think we haven't noticed it.
We have. You've hardly touched your plate,
or listened to the rest of us.
For God's sake, can't that message wait?

You're hardly the Prime Minister
who needs to be in constant touch.
I feel quite sorry for your wife.
I'm sure you aren't asked out that much!

'WHAT ARE YOU WEARING?'

'What are you wearing for Annabelle's dinner?'
What am I wearing? It's five days away!
I stare at the phone. 'Not quite decided,'
I'll make up my mind, and on the same day.

What am I wearing for Annabelle's dinner?
I just can't believe that's what she called for!
I'm well past caring what guests are wearing,
and how can she plan it five days before?

KEEP YOUR DISTANCE

Other cooks who stand beside me
and watching everything I do
will always make me do it wrong
and put me right off cooking too.

I know they're simply interested
in what I'm doing; that is true.
But still, I don't like hoverers.
I just can't cope with them. Can you?

When watched, I know I'll make a bosh.
I'd rather just get on with it.
I know you're there to give support.
That's nice – but feels the opposite!

INHERITANCE TAX

Worst subject when asked out to dine –
avoiding tax before we're dead.
If people ever bring it up,
I long to be at home in bed.

The assets we may have, or not,
and what to do before we go –
worst subject round a table, that,
and why would people want to know?

Money – best kept off the menu,
the dullest subject to discuss.
Please, what you do is up to you.
Don't share it with the rest of us!

SNOB'S CHARTER

'Serviette', 'cruets', 'lounge', 'couch',
and 'condiments' headed the words
we kids couldn't say.
And 'gob', 'grub' and 'gateau'
and worst of all, 'doilies'.
Gosh, thank the Lord
we're less snobbish today!

TEATIME

A friend of mine was none too chuffed
when all her children said 'I'm stuffed!'
the day they came around for tea
(although it didn't worry me).
She told her daughters and her son
'Oh children, please, it's just not done
to use a common, crass expression.
It always gives the wrong impression!'
And after that, they didn't stay –
she whisked all four of them away
as soon as they had finished tea,
because of their vocabulary.

MARIANNE KOENIG

She doesn't need to cook from books.
Her recipes come from her head.
The most original of cooks –
you're guaranteed to be well-fed.
A sheer delight to see her food,
and that's before you even eat it.
And when you do, you know at once
there's little chance you'll ever beat it.

SUSAN PAICE

My sister, so of course I'm biased,
but I can say quite truthfully
that few can entertain like her
and do so with such jollity.
Laughter's there, above all else,
with guaranteed good company,
and what's on every plate is great –
the perfect double recipe.

LINDA MARGERISON

Twelve folk round the table doesn't faze her,
and neither does the most ambitious meal.
How she entertains is quite amazing –
so relaxed and easy, it's unreal.
Thanks, dear Linda and your husband David,
for all those marvellous meals we've had with you.
How you cook for such a lot of people
amazes me when dining with you two.

ANOTHER ONE FOR CYD BARKER

A best friend and terrific cook is Cyd,
who never seems to make the same thing twice.
To tell the truth, I often wish she would
as everything she's cooked before is nice!

A GREAT COOK, BUT...

Never go shopping with Eva.
A trip takes all day if you do.
She has to know where food comes from,
the whole of its history too.

Never go shopping with Eva,
as she wants to know where things grow,
and what conditions they've grown in.
It can take a whole day or so.

Never go shopping with Eva,
or anyone so into food,
wanting to know every detail.
It's difficult not to be rude.

Never go shopping with Eva.
Behind you will be a long queue
of shoppers all seething with fury
and livid with her – *and* with you!

VIVE LA DIFFERENCE!

Shave celery? No, such a bore!
Whatever do cooks do it for?
And criss-cross sprout tops? Some cooks say
that sprouts are better cooked that way.
I have to say, I don't agree,
they quickly cook too soft for me.
And use decanters? Never mine,
not even with a decent wine.
And make my own bread sauce? I should,
but packet stuff is bloody good.
Use tablecloths? Of course, I could,
but far prefer the look of wood.
Use candelabras? No, too swish,
and if I used them, every dish
would have to be much grander too
and take a day or two to do.
And serve up port, or else liqueurs?
I've not done that for several years.
And clear up when the guests have gone
and then put the dishwasher on?
No, never ever late at night.
I'd rather do it at first light,
and never mind about the mess.
To me, it couldn't matter less.

It often so amuses me
how very different cooks can be.
We all do things our own sweet way
whatever other people say!

'DO HELP YOURSELF TO CURRY, EVERYONE. IT'S ALL HOME-MADE!'

Oh no, it's not! I passed the bin
you keep your garden rubbish in,
and there, discarding one last fag,
I noticed that the plastic bag
was stuffed with packets to the top –
all curries from the local shop.
All chicken tikka packs, that bin –
the same dish that you've just brought in.
But I won't give the game away.
The taste may though, I have to say!

TOO MUCH

Enough food there for twenty people,
although the table's laid for eight.
And now I've got an Everest –
a mountain load upon my plate.

It's funny how the slimmest host
can very often pile a plate
while quite forgetting those they've asked
may well be struggling with their weight.

It's also funny how slim hosts
all eat more than the rest of us.
We plough through food as best we can.
To eat just half – discourteous!

I'd really rather help myself,
but don't want to create a fuss.
If only people wouldn't serve
a plate that's far too much for us.

'IT'S ALL COME FROM OUR ALLOTMENT!'

Having dinner with allotment owners
can, on occasions, mildly irritate.
Vegetables take over conversation
Whenever they are put upon your plate.

No-one wants to hear their whole life stories
from seed to their fruition, day by day.
Lovely they can be, allotment owners,
but please do think of other things to say!

Keep them short and sweet, allotment stories,
or make them quicker than they often are.
And, above all, dear allotment owners,
make sure there's more than fruit juice at the bar!

TILE-TOPPED TABLES

The way these tables bounce the noise
is terrible, quite deafening.
However much you listen in,
you simply cannot hear a thing.
A huge mistake – the din they make
can ruin meals – it's quite unreal.
The surest way to frustrate guests
and spoil an otherwise great meal.

RECIPE FOR DISASTER

'This is a dish I learned on our travels.
Do hope you like it! Mongolian stew!'
I taste it. It's goat – not that amazing,
or worth discussing the whole evening through.

Nor is their trip in every last detail,
and looking at shots of places they saw.
Holiday stories can become dreary –
that's if they drag on a good hour or more.

Good recipe that, for boring one's guests –
stories of places that none of us know,
with iPads brought out, crammed full of photos,
making us all want to get up and go.

Holiday stories, fine for a while that.
That's if the stories are kept short and sweet.
Not if they drag on right through three courses.
A long travel lecture – hardly a treat!

CHARADES

Party games – my total nightmare,
especially at a supper do.
Leave me off your invitations,
if games like that appeal to you!

Normally quite extroverted,
all party games can make me freeze,
especially when the other guests
are very clearly so at ease.

AT A WINE BUFF'S DINNER PARTY

Wonderful wine, but only two glasses.
I'd rather have plonk, and drink a bit more.
Each glass a winner, not so the dinner.
Stuck there and sober, it's more than a bore.

Wonderful wine, and no doubt expensive,
and tasted with pomp, as most fine wines are.
Glasses soon finished – pleasure diminished,
more so, if that is the end of the bar.

Wines so expensive, host who's expansive
and boring us all on what the wines are.
He knows each chateau. Far more than we know.
Oh, for some plonk! I'd prefer that by far.

How the time passes, when all the glasses
are filled up when empty, not left to dry.
Left bereft without a single drop left,
we're longing to get up and say goodbye.

WHITEBAIT

Bill asked us round to cheer him up.
His wife has left him, suddenly.
Hours pass, and he's still cooking.
What's keeping him? I go and see.

Gosh! He's filleting the whitebait,
and sitting there, quite close to tears.
'Sainsbury said this dish was easy,
but doing this will take me years!'

I smile and scoop up all of them
and say they don't need filleting.
A lesson there for every man
who's never had to cook a thing!

'JUST BRING A BOTTLE!'

A birthday of a friend of mine:
'Don't bring a present, just some wine,
and if you truly wouldn't mind
a special one would be most kind!'

I hand it over at the door
and never see it any more.
There's wine on offer, four quid stuff!
By ten o-clock I've drunk enough.

Now what am I supposed to do?
I'd spent a bloody fortune too,
and so has every other guest.
I keep my silence like the rest.

We can't ask for our bottles back –
they're now upon our neighbour's rack.
We never guessed the crafty fella
was planning to top up his cellar.

IN MY THANKYOU CARD

'Best way, Bill, to serve up whitebait –
deep fry, until they're piping hot.
Then serve up with lemon wedges.
Too complicated, they are not!
Thanks for having me to dinner.
The whitebait tasted bloody good.
And next time darling, if you like,
I'll bring you something good for pud.'

PUDS

Anything I can do, you can do better.
Any pud you can do better than me.
My puds are dreadful, not worth a plateful.
I don't have the interest in sweet cookery.

Anything I can do, you can do better.
So don't expect puddings anyone, please!
I'm no good at cooking a sweet or a pudding –
one reason I give up and always serve cheese.

I know you would grumble if I made a crumble,
and please don't expect me to make you a tart.
Better to give up, before you all throw up,
and tell you, quite simply, I don't have the art!

'WOW!'

What a marvellous, stunning, super kitchen!
(Although I've heard she never ever cooks).
And what a stunning library in there
of seemingly unopened, glossy books!

And what a sight – those gleaming copper pans!
And what terrific AGAs! Not one, two!
Why then, are we going out as usual?
And as we always, always seem to do?

Why do people have such lavish kitchens,
but never lift a little finger there,
or get around to any entertaining?
Can't work it out at all. My brain's not there!

MY DREAM KITCHEN

What would my dream kitchen be?
A nightmare one – now that I know.
And that's a kitchen all in white
so every spill and stain will show.

What would my dream kitchen be?
In many ways the one I've got.
A clutter, yes, I must confess
but where the mess won't show a lot.

TOP FLIGHT COOKERS

Owners of the most exotic cookers
can sometimes be the most reluctant cooks.
Funny, that. I guess the top flight cookers
are sometimes bought quite simply for their looks.
Or maybe if the cooker is a top one,
then people's expectations run sky high,
scaring owners off all entertaining.
That's very probably the reason why.

Take a Woman and a Man

VALENTINE'S DAY IN A RESTAURANT

What she's thinking, what he's thinking:

How gorgeous – all these roses!
How embarrassing, all these roses.
Gosh, the place is crammed!
We'll never get served.
What an incredible menu!
Thought they'd never bring it.
I wonder how many couples here are in love?
I wonder if the other blokes are enjoying this?
If I eat any more, I'll burst.
If I drink any more, I'll never be up to it.
I wish he'd say something romantic.
Oh God, she's gone all dewy-eyed.
I wish he'd put his hand on mine.
I wish she'd take her hand off the table.
I wish he'd slip a ring on it.
I wish they'd bring the bill.
Gosh, this is lovely!
Gosh, this is agony!
I wish he'd propose.
I wish we could go home.
I'm so glad we came here.
Thank God it's only once a year.
I suppose he might propose later.
I suppose I'll have to leave a tip.
What a lovely evening!
What an amazing con!
I wonder what it cost?
I wonder if I can ask her to chip in?
Thanks, Saint Valentine!
Who was Saint Valentine, anyway?

TWO TOO MUCH FOR ME!

An Ozzie model and champ surfer.
How flattering – he fancied me!
As I did him, 'til eating out
and in a local brasserie.

He ordered a huge Porterhouse
and scoffed it in five minutes flat,
and then asked for another one!
I simply couldn't cope with that.

Ever been out with a fellow
who ate two steaks – and in a row?
I sat in utter disbelief.
A huge, tall chap – but even so!

That second steak just turned me off,
and watching him did in my brain.
Put me off him altogether.
What point in meeting up again?

A BALLAD ABOUT A SALAD

Nasturtium petals in a salad –
it seems a rather nice idea,
though men will always pick them out,
at least the chaps invited here.

The sight of petals in a salad
is something fellows cannot take,
and soon they start to pick them out
as if they fell in by mistake.

They look at them, all quizzical.
Astonished, they then look at you
and wonder if they're edible.
They never quite know what to do.

Flowers are flowers and lettuce, lettuce,
and men will always wonder whether
you've flipped and gone right off your head
when serving up the two together.

MY WIFE

'My wife asks friends to dinner,
then doesn't want to cook,
and tries to find excuses
to get her off the hook,
but then turns out a triumph
and loved the time it took.
Why ask people over,
then wish that you had not,
and then cook like an angel?
You women – funny lot.
I'll never understand you.
What crazy brains you've got!

WHEN I WAS YOUNG

When I was young, I used to wait
upon my husband, serve his plate
and fill his glass when it got dry
and listen to his every sigh.

Well, they say, how time does fly!
And now I've changed, he wonders why.
He asks me why and I reply
'We women do as time goes by!'

Yes, things are very changed today.
They've changed a lot, I have to say.
I do not wait on him all day.
Those days are very far away.

When he was young, he didn't wait
on me at all, or serve my plate
or fill my glass when it got dry
or listen to my every sigh.

He never did a household chore,
but now he does – a whole lot more,
and doesn't think that's what I'm for.
Time has evened up the score!

He helps me now, and quite a bit,
and doesn't chicken out of it.
It's often quite the opposite –
and I am simply loving it!

Metre based on 'The Bluetail Fly', an anonymous American song

'I DON'T UNDERSTAND YOU WOMEN.'

'I go to buy a spanner,
and end up with just that.
My wife shops for a saucepan
and ends up with a hat.
And now she doesn't like it.
Are women all like that?'

RECIPE

Take a woman and a man.
Sprinkle her liberally with rose petals,
blossoms of jasmine, and fine French wine.
(Champagne may also be used).

To him, add spices, sauce and red-hot pepper.
Whisk constantly.
Blend until smooth; there should be no lumps.
Allow to bubble for two years at maximum heat –
the top should be frothy with golden peaks.

Add a baby and stir.

Gradually remove all other ingredients, and
simmer at low temperature for a further two years.

Allow to cool.

Now, take a sharp knife and slice in two.

THE CURSE OF CAPABILITY

The trouble, if you're 'capable' –
you don't get fancy things.
You're given a new casserole
but never diamond rings.

The more you do, the less men do
in matters of the heart,
that soft embrace or single rose –
they soon forget the art.

'You're good at that!' they say to you.
You are – so carry on –
until the day it dawns on you
their tenderness has gone.

The trouble, if you're 'capable' –
you watch while other wives
who cannot do a bloody thing
lead more romantic lives.

'My husband has just bought me this!'
They twirl, in some new dress,
or show me a new Prada bag.
That irks, I must confess.

And if you also earn your keep,
well, then it's even worse.
You'll dine out yes, but only Dutch,
he'll empty half your purse.

The more we do, the less they do
in matters of the heart –
the answer is to do much less,
and do that from the start!

'DAD, MUM'S JUST LEFT YOU.'

'What? She can't have!' 'Well, she has, Dad.
She says you're married to your club.'
'And has she left me any dinner?'
'No.' 'What? Not left me any grub?'

True story that. A great friend's Dad
had not got past the front door mat
before he spouted out those words.
His marriage ended, just like that.

MY HUSBAND AT THE CONNAUGHT

'Why are you so pale, my darling?
Are you feeling ill?
What makes you so pale, my dearest?
Do you need a pill?

My goodness darling, what is wrong?
Tell me, are you ill?
What's made you so deathly pale, dear?'
'Looking at the bill.'

ME AT THE CONNAUGHT

At times, I find there comes a day
I don't care what we have to pay
for going to a restaurant.
At times, all cooks feel put upon!

'DON'T FORGET TOMORROW, LIZ!'

'Why? What's tomorrow?' 'Dinner here.
I told you – supper here at eight.'
(Oh God, I'm going somewhere else.
Now, who to cancel? And so late?)

LOVE LETTER

My darling,
I'm in love. It was a 'coup de foudre'. I adore your strength,
your character, the touch and feel of you, your presence, your
steeliness, your stature. I knew at once I couldn't live without
you, that we could never be parted. And I can't wait for your
arrival. I am wishing the days away. There has always been a
void in my life, a hole waiting to be filled. Now we will be
together for always. In love, in harmony, inseparable. A union
made in heaven. Darling AGA, what a looker, what a cooker!
The greatest love,
Lucy XXX

'WHEN'S DINNER?'

'When's dinner, Liz?' 'When you cook it.'
'But I can't cook!' 'It's time to try.
Or take me out. I've gone on strike.
I need a break.' I hear him sigh.
'But what to cook?' 'Look in the fridge.'
'But where's the fridge? Remind me where.'
He wanders off, dejectedly.
I look at him and in despair.

SELECTIVE DEAFNESS

He reads the papers. I wash up.
I bang and clatter every pan.
But does he ever get the hint?
Selective deafness, that's my man!

ANOTHER FINE MESS

Why can't he make a single slice of toast
without me clearing all the crumbs away?
Why can't he put the lid back on the jam?
Why do I have to do it every day?

Why is it me who puts the butter back
and wipes the surfaces, and yet again?
Why does he always treat me like a maid?
I guess that's true of many, many men.

Thank God his virtues well outweigh his faults.
In fact, not clearing up – his only one.
I guess I'll have to live with daily mess,
because at other times, he's such good fun.

I'm looking at a dirty plate right now,
and only inches from the kitchen sink.
I'll wash it up, and as I always do –
but he could do that too, and in a wink!

CURIOUS

The girlfriend of a friend of ours
would never eat leftover stuff.
If things weren't eaten, all were thrown –
until the poor chap had enough.

All was chucked into the dustbin
if not consumed – and there and then.
But why did he put up with that?
Too tolerant – the best of men.

She's now back in Romania,
still phoning him and every day,
but he will never have her back,
not throwing all that food away.

'It cost a mint and left me skint,
and in the end, quite furious.
Refusing all leftover food?
Liz, don't you find that curious?'

'SUCH A GREAT HOST, BUT...'

'He rushes round attending to the glasses.
He hands round dishes, quite the perfect host.
He clears the plates and puts them on the sideboard,
and then, meal over, offers me a toast.

But otherwise, he never lifts a finger.
I do it all.' I say that I do too,
(adding that my man does next to nothing
when giving any kind of dinner do).

Best I think to look at all their good points.
With luck, your chap (like mine) will have a few.
Best to button up on their shortcomings.
They'll quickly find a whole lot more in you!

BLUNT CARVING KNIVES

How often do you sharpen knives?
That's something that I never do.
If husbands very rarely cook,
why should they leave it up to you?

I'm blunt with mine, when knives are too.
I think he ought to do that task.
Well, if your old man doesn't cook,
it's surely not too much to ask.

And if your fellow likes to carve
(it seems to me, that most men do)
then surely sharpening the knives
is one small way of thanking you!

SHORT NOTICE

'*WHAT*! You've asked six people round for dinner?'
'Yes, they're lovely – met them yesterday.
Lovely people, met them at the jazz club.
Said we'd have them round – in fact, today.'

'*WHAT*? You've asked them round *tonight*? For dinner?'
'Well, make it simple. That's what I would do.'
'Only thing *I'll* do is lay the table,
and then, my darling, leave it up to you.

Well, *you* asked them. I don't feel like cooking.'
'But I can't cook!' 'Yes darling, that I know.
Best get started, you will think of something –
it's four o'clock, there's not much time to go.'

A BREAK IS AS GOOD AS A FEAST

Suddenly, you've gone off cooking.
I think that's pretty commonplace.
It's nice to have friends round to eat,
but suddenly you need your space.
Then your old man goes and tells you
he's asked some friends to come and stay,
exactly when you want a break –
and need a cooking holiday.

AUTUMN LEAVES

It's awfully bad luck on my husband,
the fellow is married to me,
as while I am clearing the garden,
for him there is little time free.

Right now we are living on pizzas,
or cold things are shoved on his plate.
He's longing to have a hot dinner.
At least there is not long to wait.

Just let him take over the cooking?
The last thing that I'd ever do.
Scrambled eggs, that's all he can manage.
He's never learned anything new.

This autumn has been quite a bummer
for making him anything hot.
It's awfully bad luck on my husband
that a cook he is patently not.

We could always go to a restaurant,
but then, that would cost us the earth,
though pizzas he now has to live on
are not doing much for his girth.

He needs to be several pounds lighter.
It's going the opposite way.
His trousers are very much tighter.
The zips hardly do up today.

It's awfully bad luck on my husband.
Thank goodness, the end is in sight.
I told him, and only this morning,
'I'm cooking a topside tonight!'

BURDEN

Cooking – in a way, a daily burden,
an endless challenge thinking what to do,
and avoiding too much repetition.
I find it tough at times, perhaps like you.

Cooking for our friends can be delightful,
but when it's for survival, often not.
That can be a chore, and bloody boring,
the downside of our cooking such a lot.

Don't you yearn, at times, for cooking freedom,
a time to put your pots and pans away?
Maybe that's the biggest single reason
cooks love to go away on holiday.

JOKERS AT THE TABLE

'Have you heard the one about the golf club?'
Oh no, can't bear it, not another joke.
It's not that I can't bear jokes at the table,
but strings of them can put me off a bloke.
Worried that I might not get the ending –
that doesn't help, nor knowing when to laugh.
Anecdotes and stories, so much better,
especially when they're from my other half.
Raconteur he is, and such a great one,
I've heard his stories loads of time before.
Still I laugh until I'm almost crying.
One reason why I married him? For sure!

Bake-Off

BAKE-OFF

Bake-off; huge hit, watched by millions,
although the programme's not for me.
What a star is Mary Berry
attracting such publicity!

But one thing always puzzles me.
Who finds the time for eating cake
and all of those exotic things
that people on the programme bake?

All cake – for me, that goes with tea.
But who's at home that time of day?
Just when do people find a slot
to put that kind of food away?

A MASTERCHEF MOAN

'I'm sometimes sad that I won Masterchef.'
'Why?' 'Nobody invites us any more,
thinking that they have to meet my standards.'
'But do you wish you *hadn't* won?' 'For sure.'
'Goodness me, are people that neurotic?'
'I'm sad to say so, but I think they are.
I always say I'm happy with things simple,
but people feel they have to raise the bar.
'Jane and I, these days we feel quite lonely.
Now, each and every night, it's just us two.
No-one asks us round, not any longer.
It's getting pretty rare when any do.'

COME DINE WITH ME.'

A programme that amazes me.
Incredible what people do
when asked into a stranger's house.
Go through their wardrobes? Gosh, would you?

And what they wear and what they say
is truly quite astonishing.
I hope they bring the series back.
I've always found it riveting.

Of course, the programme makers know
that guests from hell make great TV,
and courtesy in dinner guests
is not what people want to see.

I admit, I'm quite embarrassed
admitting that I love that show –
mostly as the people on it
are not like anyone I know.

But one thing I don't watch it for
is new ideas preparing food.
No, it's simply people's manners.
How can they be so bloody rude?

IN A SMART FISH RESTAURANT

When Ben remarked his fish was off
(the most amenable of men)
the Maitre 'D said it was fresh
and Ben said, 'Yes, it was. But *when?*'

THE COUPLE BY OUR SIDE

They never said a single thing –
the couple sitting by our side.
Maybe our never-ending tide
of words was simply not their way,
and they found what they heard absurd
and wished us twenty feet away.

Perhaps they did communicate,
but in a very different way.
Or maybe they had lots to say,
but not that evening, not right then.
Or else, perhaps, the day had come
when any words were much too late,
and both had turned too deaf and dumb.

BUNYADI

(London's first naked restaurant)

Gosh, would you believe, the first nude restaurant
has opened up in London? Grisly thought!
What's more, the waiting list to go and eat there
apparently is anything but short.
Can you think of anything more ghastly
than dining out with strangers in the nude,
willies, breasts and bare bums all around you?
Quite frankly, that would put me off the food.

GASTROPUBS

Ever go to gastropubs?
Ever feel they're somewhat pseud?
Apologies to managers –
I know the following is rude.

SIX GOLDEN RULES FOR GASTROPUB STAFF

1. Use French words at every opportunity.
2. Use longer words where shorter words would do.
3. With English words, embellish, e.g. 'drizzled'; not 'poured.'
4. Do not be too convivial. Look serious. That suggests the food is.
5. Do not ask if the customers have enjoyed their meal. Assume they have.
6. Ask them if there is anything else they would like to see on the menu. That suggests we may actually do something about it.

WHAT'S WRONG WITH PLATES?

A starter on a pebble, a main course on a slate.
It seems, in top class restaurants, it's out of date; a plate.
And if you ever get one, you're given one that's square –
exactly like an ashtray. That's something I can't bear!
But ask them for a round plate? Oh no, that would be rude,
though thinking about fag ends quite puts me off the food.

'LE RANQUET', TORNAC

A five-star restaurant in France –
I shouldn't really give its name,
but with a waiter quite so rude
it only has itself to blame.

Courtesy flew off the menu
just minutes after sitting down.
What diners choose and what they do
should surely not make waiters frown.

I dropped a breadcrumb on the plate –
a huge gold one in front of me,
purely there for decoration.
My goodness, how he scowled at me!

And then, when ordering our wine –
the horrid fellow smirked at us.
It wasn't from the pricy end,
but smirk? Oh, how discourteous!

Things did not get that much better.
The cooking wasn't even great,
with tiny and pretentious things
for which we had to wait – and wait.

Did we tip? I can't remember.
And if we did, then silly us.
I'm pretty sure we didn't though,
because we left so furious.

Last year, the restaurant closed down –
a high price for pretentiousness.
But even if the food's five star,
good manners do not matter less.

THE DEATH OF LA GRANDE RUE

Close up at twelve, most French shops do.
You can't buy food from twelve to two
(except, of course, in restaurants).
At mid-day, shops stop serving you.
The shutters go up at mid-day.
The clock strikes twelve, shops go on strike,
so crucial is that mid-day meal –
one thing in France I don't much like!

NOTICE ON OUR COFFEE PERCOLATOR IN FRANCE

*DEAR ALL, DON'T SWISH GRAINS DOWN THE DRAIN.
YOU WON'T BE ASKED TO STAY AGAIN.
PLEASE NOTE – THEY'RE THIN, THE PIPES IN FRANCE.
JUST POUR THE GRAINS OUTSIDE ON PLANTS!*

It's lovely that you've come to stay,
but sadly, you may have to pay
for ripping up our floors and drains
if swishing down your coffee grains!

And leaving me to clean the pot,
I have to say, my friends, is not
a job I like to do each day
while you lot scamper off to play!

THE FRENCH AND THE ENGLISH ARE DIVIDED BY A LOT MORE THAN A STRIP OF SEA.

Like many people, I grow mint.
And so, I'm pretty sure, do you.
What's more, I'd never serve up lamb
without at least a sprig or two.

And yes, of course I'll make a sauce –
it goes with lamb so perfectly,
although the French would not agree –
they'd see that as a travesty.

Mint with lamb – to Brits, delicious,
and mint with spuds, that's hard to beat,
but if you have a Gallic nose,
two dishes that you'd never eat.

Serve mint with meat? *'Non. Dégoûlasse!'*
And mint with spuds? *'C'ést barbarie!'*
Our two nations are divided
by far more than a strip of sea.

A mint patch – here a common sight,
but not in *'potagers'* in France.
And as for serving lamb with mint?
Across the Channel, not a chance!

JEAN-PIERRE

To say that little Jean-Pierre
displayed a certain cooking flair
was quite to understate a boy
to whom 'cuisine' was purest joy.

His 'gigot d'agneau' was 'superbe',
so too, his 'omelettes fines herbes',
and as for ways with 'pommes de terres'
and 'soupes' and 'pâté fèrmiere'
and quite stupendous apple 'tarte',
you couldn't but admire his art!
The greatest chefs would be impressed,
indeed, the finest and the best,
like Stein, Le Blanc and Michel Roux,
who share a 'Michelin' or two.

However, though a gifted child,
he drove his poor old Maman wild.
No meal she made was good enough,
The 'jus' too thick, 'viande' too tough,
the 'coq au vin' too highly spiced,
the 'gateau' incorrectly sliced.

One day, attacked for scorching 'boeuf',
she cried out, 'Jean! Un 'oeuf's' un 'oeuf!'
I'm sick and tired of washing up
each knife and fork and dish and cup
and messy, sticky pot and pan.
It's high time you did that, young man!
I hate you saying 'Dégoulasse',
and calling all my cuisine crass.
You may well make a fine 'roulade',
but, 'Mon Dieu, fils', you make life hard!
You never say my food is 'bon,'
as would a kind and nice 'garçon'!

PAS POUR MOI!

While loving almost all things French,
there is one custom that I hate.
Why can't they leave their knives and forks
together on an emptied plate?

Left sideways, not a pretty sight,
and clearing up is harder too.
Why is that customary in France?
One thing I wish they wouldn't do!

BARRY'S COMPLAINT

'Roast woodchuck served with juniper –
that kind of food just isn't me.
Steak and frites – great – now you're talking!
All haute cuisine, too haute for me.
The word 'haute' now sticks in my throat,
the whole thing's got right out of hand.
'Basse cuisine' – that's far more like it,
with dishes I can understand.
Give me pies and sausages,
and puddings, not a chic dessert.
Not for me, those fancy dishes
at prices all so high, they hurt.'
Dear Barry, such a heathen, he,
although I have some sympathy.
At times, 'haute' is too haute for me,
especially served pretentiously.

SNAILS

I used to love them in my youth,
but never will eat snails again;
not after seeing their insides
when stuck upon a window pane.
Awful sight inside each belly –
it put me off the escargot.
A beastly, frilly, jelly mélée.
I've not had one since years ago.
And as for porridge made with snails;
that's my idea of utter hell.
Gosh, do people really eat that
and think that they are dining well?

GUESTS ABROAD

Some prefer a long, protracted breakfast
that starts round ten and lasts until mid-day –
brunchers, who then irritate the lunchers
(who often have to clear their mess away).
Early birds and late ones can mean warfare
when it comes to eating out of doors,
often making people pretty grumpy.
Different body clocks – a major cause.

NOUVELLE CUISINE RESTAURANTS

Teeny weeny little portions
at prices just the opposite.
Nouvelle cuisine? No, not my scene.
I'm far too mean to pay for it!
A delicacy on each dish,
and all served up with great panache,
such works of art, prepared with heart,
but never, I think, worth the cash.
Yes, less can certainly mean more,
and often does with such cuisine.
The prices can be far, far more,
especially when the portion's mean.

'I LIKE THE BRITS, THEY DO NOT EAT US.'

(Seen on a shopping bag in France,
with a picture of happy frogs)

'I like the Brits, they do not eat us.'
Seen on a bag of Calvados.
I'm rather glad we don't eat frogs,
although the French think that's our loss.

I'm most relieved we don't eat frogs.
Of frogs I've always been most fond,
and few things beat the sight and sound
of hundreds croaking in a pond.

IN FLORIDA

Surf and turf? No, not together.
And worse – a great big plate of it.
No way, when in the USA
I'll like that. Quite the opposite.

I like the surf, and like the turf,
but not together on a plate.
And not so much! *Please*, not so much!
An overcrowded plate I hate!

NOTICE IN A NEW YORK PIZZA PARLOUR –

Are you fairly hungry? Very hungry? Super hungry? Tell us!

I told them I was super hungry.
(I hadn't eaten on the plane).
The pizza was enough for twelve.
I've learned not to say that again!
The pizza – almost two feet wide,
four times the size of Dominos.
How can New Yorkers get through that?
How *can* they fit it in? God knows!

CHINESE RESTAURANTS

Ordering a choice of dishes –
that's normal here in the UK.
But watch out if you're in Hong Kong.
You'll soon be pushing bowls away.
Each one can be enough for two,
and four's too many, that's for sure.
It won't be long before you're full
and cannot fit a mouthful more.

EXOTIC FOOD HOLIDAYS

Anyone for chocolate-coated locusts?
And anyone for balls of kangaroo?
What about a funky stew of monkey?
Who goes on faddy food trips? Many do.

Loads of ads now fill the Sunday papers.
It sounds quite pleasant, all the scenery.
But sushi made of slugs and local pond weed?
That's simply not my kind of recipe!

Who can stomach all those crazy prices?
It doesn't add up, the arithmetic –
not if eating food that you're not used to,
with every chance you'll end up feeling sick.

Post-Mortems

TURKISH DELIGHT

Delightful, mine was firmly not.
The pan, I think, got far too hot.
Yuk! The taste was most unpleasant.
Not the nicest Christmas present.

At times, it's best to buy the stuff –
especially confectionery,
and Christmas time is not the time
to try a complex recipe.

The thought was nice, the taste was not.
Delightful? No, the opposite.
And now I'll have to chuck the pan,
with all that goo burned into it.

PLEASE, NO MORE MUGS FOR CHRISTMAS!

Where has all the shelf space gone?
Long time passing.
Where has all the shelf space gone,
long time ago?

Where has every inch all gone?
Under mugs, and every one.
All gifts I can't return.
When will the family learn?

CHRISTMAS

I've wrapped all the gifts, I've put up the tree,
I've hung up the cards – he's on the first tee.

I've made the mince pies, I've done the bread sauce –
he's off playing golf, it's par for the course.

I've mended the lights, I've basted the duck –
he's now in a bunker bemoaning his luck.

I've worked out the table, we're having fourteen.
I've polished the silver – he's now on the green.

I've hung up the wreath, it's on the front door –
he's on the sixteenth, he'll do it in four.

At six, he'll be back, poor over-tired soul,
and I'll have to listen to hole after hole.

I'll smile when he says, 'The day was quite fun.'
But not when he asks, 'And what have you done?'

WHAT TO DO WITH LEFTOVER TURKEY?

What the hell to do with turkey
that's not used up on Christmas Day,
or else on Boxing Day, alas?
You can't just chuck the lot away.

Now, turkey pilaff? Curry? Soup?
Or turkey salad? Turkey hash?
Turkey slivers with glass noodles?
Cold turkey with a parsley mash?

Turkey stew or Coronation?
Or turkey with an orange sauce?
Turkey gratin served with almonds?
A turkey mayo starter course?

No – turkey stock, the only thing.
(That's if your pans are big enough).
After two days eating turkey
most people just can't face the stuff.

And even if you do make stock,
your freezer may be clogged for years,
with quite enough for endless soup
to bore your dinner guests to tears.

And if it weren't for Christmas Day,
when would we bother with this bird?
Even humble chicken dishes
are likely to be far preferred.

BABES IN ARMS – AND RESTAURANTS

Highchairs in a lovely restaurant –
that's something I don't want to see.
I don't mind children in the place
but not a tot in infancy.

Highchairs always lower romance,
especially if babes start to cry,
as do prams and Moses baskets.
Why take tots out? I wonder why.

Well, maybe as the au pair's off,
and parents feel they need a break.
But so do we, oh so do we!
Don't bring the babe for heaven's sake!

We're parents too, and just like you,
but adults who prefer to eat
with other adults where they dine,
and don't find nurseries a treat.

We know how very proud you are,
but don't display that publicly,
at least, not in a stylish place.
We'd rather they were infant-free.

NOTHING MORE THAN BUNGING IN A TURKEY

'Nothing more than bunging in a turkey.'
My husband says that each and every year.
I try and point out, every single Christmas,
it's not as easy as it may appear.
'Thirteen things to cook is not that easy,
especially when the whole lot must be hot.'
And if he says it one more time, I'll tell him
'You do it all, as this year I will not!'
Only bunging turkey in an oven?
It's time we women left it all to men,
then sat back and watched a sheer disaster.
They'd soon ask us to do it all again!

SEXY FOOD

Food sexy? Yes, apparently.
And also how you eat it, too.
The internet has lots of tips
on sexy dining out for two.

But I'm a bit too old for that.
The whole idea of sexy meals
is better left to younger folk,
however young inside one feels!

YOUR LOCAL

What used to be your splendid pub
is now a mum and baby club –
with buggies, buggies everywhere –
there's one stuck right behind your chair.
And breasts on show, that's also true –
you often get a flash or two
when someone's feeding time is due.
Can't say I like it much. Do you?

What used to be an adult place
has now become a toddler space,
where all the infants Mums bring in
create the most obnoxious din
with bells and rattles drowning out
the things you want to talk about –
and babies often crying, too.
Can't say I like it much. Do you?

And if tots have a screaming fit
and you say, 'Walk them round a bit,
and better still, not here – outside.'
Well that 's a knock to Mummy's pride.
She'll snap, 'DON'T TELL ME WHAT TO DO!'
Can't say I like it much. Do you?

SHELLING PEAS IN CHILDHOOD

Back then, when shelling peas,
it never was much fun,
as maggots lived in pods –
and almost every one.

Disgusting, shelling peas.
It quite revolted me,
with nasty squirming babes
surrounding every pea.

And put peas in your mouth?
Well, rather you than me.
But maybe pods you shelled
were lots less maggoty.

You may be half my age,
and never seen a pod
with maggots curled inside.
Those days have gone, thank God.

AUTUMN YEARS

Season of depth, new-found contentedness,
close bosom friend of many women now,
conspiring with them how to worry less
about the tiny crow's feet on the brow,
and how to fill the days with merry laughter,
and fill more nights with friends around to sup,
and care much less about the morning after,
and wait 'til then to do the washing up.
Season of calm and new-found sisterhood,
no enemy of any woman now,
no lies, betrayals, no conspiracies,
no other woman hissing, 'Bloody cow'!

Metre from 'Ode to Autumn' by John Keats

AN ANCIENT PROBLEM

Awful thing when guests get older –
you have to think of people's teeth.
Maybe dentures in the top row,
and probably some more beneath.

What to give them? Nothing chewy.
So many dishes you can't do,
things they'd find a dental challenge.
If I were you, I'd make a stew.

LE CREUSET

Marvellous casseroles, Le Creuset,
but heavier, and by the year.
They weigh a ton, that's not much fun
when cooking for a crowd round here.

Try filling them with food for ten
and lift or move them if you can.
Wow, they're heavy and unwieldy –
you need the strength of Superman.

Not too good for older shoulders,
but gorgeous-looking, that's for sure.
I have to say I dread the day
I just can't lift them any more.

P.S.
In fact, alas, that day has come.
I'm sitting here, and in a sling.
Broken shoulder, frightful fracture.
I now can't lift a bloody thing!

PEELING SPUDS

For years before I used a peeler,
I simply used a kitchen knife.
And with a peeler (so much faster)
I also bought myself a life.
For years we don't discover things
(or maybe it is only me
who takes so long to find things out
that peel hours from our cookery).

HOSTESS TROLLEYS

Remember them? Once all the rage.
In fact, I'd rather like one here.
But now considered naff, of course,
although a rather good idea.
To keep food hot is challenging
(and often more than cooking is).
What a shame that hostess trolleys
are now thought great vulgarities!
Why do people find things vulgar,
and all at once, and just like that?
What makes useful new inventions
quite suddenly seem so old hat?

GALA DINNERS

Awful if they use round tables.
You only hear guests next to you.
That's if you're getting on a bit
and don't hear as you used to do.
And, if those on each side of you
are talking to their left and right,
you're left marooned, embarrassed too,
and wishing you'd not gone that night.
And if they're bores, you've got just cause
to go before the speech is due.
Perhaps it's very rude of me,
but that is what I've learned to do.
Over sixty? Save your money,
or send it to the charity,
unless your hearing's bloody good.
Those gala evenings – misery!

THE THROWAWAY GENERATION

'What's this, Mum?' Half a pack of bacon
is quickly tossed into the rubbish bin.
Its 'best by' date was only yesterday.
With youngsters now, my patience can wear thin.

Chuckers, throwers, 'eat by' date fanatics.
Why can't our children simply use their eyes?
Or use their noses, or their common-sense?
These days, if any do, it's a surprise.

Out goes a cabbage with one leaf that's yellow
and out go things that could make soup or sauce.
Don't they ever think about the wastage?
No point in ever asking that of course.

Victims, most, of supermarket sales ploys.
The more we chuck, the better they will do.
How many children question labelling?
Annoyingly, I'd say it's very few.

'AUNTIE'S LEG' OR 'GRANNY'S ARM'

That's suet pud by any other name,
but eating it would never be the same
without those childhood titles we were taught –
both apt, although a truly grisly thought.

'Auntie's leg' or 'Granny's arm'– revolting,
although it rarely puts kids off the pud.
Children seem to love such grisly titles.
Without one, suet pud's not half as good!

MY FAVOURITE ROALD DAHL STORY

She killed her husband with a leg of lamb,
and frozen hard, it split apart his head.
And when the police had been there many hours,
she said 'It's surely time that you were fed.
Why not stay, and I can make you dinner?
Well, doesn't that makes perfect common-sense?'
The police agreed, and ate up all the lamb,
quite unaware they'd scoffed the evidence.

AT THE CHECK-OUT

Our trolley – as usual, crammed full of wine.
'Having a party?' the check-out girl said.
'No.' says my husband. 'Oh!' says the poor girl,
avoiding our faces, her own going red.

All conversation dies in an instant.
Maybe it's kinder to tell her a lie,
or perhaps wiser not to ask shoppers
the reason for things they've chosen to buy.

PORFIRIO RUBIROSA

Why are huge red-pepper grinders
called 'Rubirosas'? Very crude.
If people ask, I rarely say.
To do so might be rather rude!
Famous grinder, Rubirosa,
and with, it's said, a massive dong.
If I said that over dinner,
I think some guests would not stay long.
Barbara Hutton (Woolworth heiress)
was Rubirosa's squeeze in bed,
although I don't expand on that –
some things are better left unsaid.
Doris Duke, as rich as Croesus,
was Rubirosa's middle wife.
Both gave him a Mitchell bomber
before they axed him from their life.
Why, I ask, a Mitchell bomber?
And what a strange coincidence!
And how much did those bombers cost?
I hate to think of the expense.
There was a time when waiters smiled
when grinding pepper on your plate,
while never saying why they smiled,
but none of them do that of late.
These days, not many people know
a thing about Porfirio.
I sometimes wish that *I* did not.
Some things are better *not* to know!

THE PALEOLITHIC DIET

Vegans – tough enough to cook for.
Thank goodness no-one that I know
is into a big diet craze
that followers call 'Paleo.'

Lots of protein – that's allowed,
but dairy products firmly aren't,
and nor are legumes, beans and grains.
And put out peanuts? No, you can't.

Fans into 'micronutrients'
(or into any trendy fad)
would not enjoy my sort of food.
I find the whole thing somewhat sad.

How awful when asked out to dine
to phone with all forbidden food.
That's such a strain on any host.
On top of that, it's somewhat rude.

The list of things they cannot eat
takes both sides of several pages.
Just ploughing through forbidden foods
takes you absolutely ages.

You may well know a 'paleo'.
I have to say I'm glad I don't.
It's not for me, that caveman grub
and cook for 'paleos', I won't!

OMNIVORE

I'm often grateful I'm an omnivore.
How dull to eat the same thing every day.
How boring for a cow or hungry horse
condemned to live each day on grass or hay.

And how appalling life must be for cows
that have to eat a mass of grass each day,
as grass is pretty short of nutrients,
and if they didn't, they would fade away.

I'm also grateful I'm a Westerner.
I have to say, I wouldn't find it nice
to have to eat the same food every day –
and most of all, if that was always rice.

Rice, I've always thought is pretty boring.
What does it taste of? Nothing much to me.
Fills me up. What else to recommend it?
Well, nothing else as far as I can see.

A GOOD HAMMERING

All toddlers like to hammer things,
especially a boiled egg top.
That's what makes a boiled egg smashing.
A shame to ask a kid to stop.

Slice the top off? Do it for them?
I wouldn't want to spoil their fun.
I let them hammer all they like,
but make sure yolks are overdone!

'DAD, YOU'RE SUCH A PHILISTINE!'

'All you seem to want is toast and Marmite.
Gosh, don't you ever like a decent meal?'
'Frankly, not that much. Most stuff's too fancy.
And all those cooking programmes – they're unreal.'

'Perhaps it was those years of army grub
that made you such a foodie heathen, Dad.
Such a shame you don't take Mum to restaurants.
I have to say, I find that rather sad.'

'Waste of money, eating out in restaurants,
I can't think why so many people do.
And I'm sure your mother doesn't miss it.'
I don't reply, but doubt his words are true.

JOSH JENSEN

A friend of ours from California
who owns a well-known winery,
and flies to London every year
for reasons of publicity.

Wine tastings, always great events
when fellow growers gather there,
and chefs we often recognise –
familiar faces everywhere.

And afterwards, and best of all,
they get a restaurant's permission
to take in scores of different wines
left over from the exhibition.

Then, when new diners come on in,
my goodness, how they stop and stare
to see our table crammed with wines –
and different labels everywhere!

They stop and gape with open mouths.
How much, they wonder, has that cost?
But Josh and us – we don't let on.
No, so much pleasure would be lost!

JOHN AND COLIN – MY FATHER AND UNCLE

When greedy John was offered cake,
the largest slice he'd always take.
With just two slices on the plate,
my father, John, would never wait
to see if his sweet older brother
might well, perhaps, prefer the other.
Said Colin, 'John, it's just not nice
you always pick the larger slice.
Your manners, brother, do appal one.
If it were me, I'd pick the small one.
Said naughty John, 'Then why complain
you've got the smaller slice again?
Don't moan to me about your lot,
as what you want, is what you've got!'

(My Dad, however, was a General.
His brother, though, a gentle priest.
That, perhaps, may well explain things.
It does a bit – to me, at least).

REPETITION KILLS APPETITE

Eat too much of any food
and suddenly there comes a day
you can't stand one more bite of it
and (if you can) shove plates away.
Boarding schools can do that for you
as mine did many years ago,
and pilchards, yuk, still top the list
of foods that I don't want to know.
And semolina I can't face.
At school, we had that every day –
every day in different colours
to take monotony away.
Rabbit – cheap in post-war Britain –
another thing that I eschew.
We simply ate too much of it,
along with things like Irish stew.
Old-fashioned things, now coming back –
like tripe and gizzards, brawn and brain,
but count me out of eating them.
I won't touch things like that again!

PECTIN

Make jam? Why not? But will it set?
That's very easy to forget.
The pectin is supposed to jell,
but doesn't always do that well.
And mostly, jam turns into juice.
Why bother then? That's my excuse!

POOF!

The season of the barbecue –
charred smells and all through summer too.
You truly long to eat out there,
but not with that smell in the air.
A gorgeous sunny day out there,
but not with that stench everywhere!
The neighbour's barbecue – you groan.
Your garden is a no-go zone.

ESTATE AGENTS

'Everyone today wants good-sized kitchens,
and even if the buyers rarely cook.
And what they also want is lack of clutter.
Um, could you tidy yours before they look?'

Ours – crammed with memorabilia –
the opposite of minimal.
Oh well, what if we never sell?
I find a cram more beautiful.

To me, a mass of family things
gives kitchens loads of character.
I'd rather see a place like that,
but not one agent would concur.

Can't people see beyond the junk
and visualise how things might be?
It seems they can't – it fazes them.
But why? To me, a mystery.

CYD AND SYD'S KITCHEN

A kitchen where I love to be,
and one that everybody likes –
a kitchen like a gallery
with paintings done by Sydney Sykes.
A bowl of mussels, garlic string,
a single lemon, or a pear,
a bunch of beetroots, broccoli –
such lovely paintings everywhere.
Before you even start to eat,
you get such pleasure from his art,
and when Cyd cooks (his other half),
her talents also lift the heart.
Want a painting for your kitchen?
Here's how to get in touch with Syd.
There's one thing I can promise you;
you'll be extremely glad you did!

sydney.sykes@btinternet.com

A KNOCK TO HIS PRIDE

A wine buff came to dinner – a chap called Cyril Ray,
an expert on the subject (and sadly, dead today).

We served a splendid claret – a name among the best,
and happily he loved it and seemed to be impressed.

And then, for the dessert course,
we changed to something white,
and watched old Cyril beaming –
'I'm glad I came tonight!

My favourite – Château d'Yquem! How very kind of you!'
But was it Château d'Yquem? Er, no, that wasn't true.

Our choice was far more humble – home-made elderflower,
but Cyril sat there beaming at least another hour.

He studied it, the bottle,
surprised to see no label,
and sighed when it was empty
and taken from the table.

And then my husband blew it (a much too honest bloke),
and sadly poor old Cyril did not enjoy the joke.

'It's elderflower, Cyril! We picked it from outside!'
Disaster – he was livid. A huge knock to his pride.

He had a reputation – an expert, he was vain,
and promptly left the table and never came again.

*This is a true story, although the home-made elderflower wine wasn't served by my husband, but my father-in-law,
the wicked Toby O'Brien, fond of a practical joke. Cyril Ray was a famous wine writer for The Sunday Times.*

HOW LOVELY!

How nice to get a card, not just an email
to thank me for a supper party here!
I've pinned it to my kitchen notice board
where it may stay at least another year.

Cards, so thoughtful, always more than welcome,
but getting them these days is somewhat rare.
Sad, as cards are always worth the effort,
and emails (though they're nice) just can't compare.

THE MORNING AFTER

Last night, our best friends came to dinner.
They left at a quarter past two.
But what did we say to each other?
It's dreadful, I haven't a clue.

I'm sure that the evening was lovely.
I'm certain it went with a swing.
But what did we say round the table?
I barely remember a thing.

I seem to recall that we argued,
but what did we argue about?
It can't have been all that important.
Perhaps I should call to find out.

The saucepans are pleasingly empty,
There's nothing much left of the pud.
Did no-one once mention the dinner,
and say that my cooking was good?

Perhaps we've met rather too often,
and said all the same things before.
Perhaps we said nothing that mattered,
or can't hear as well any more.

It must have been pleasantly jolly –
the bottles give that much away.
But what in God's name did we talk of?
Whatever did anyone say?

'THANKS!'

'Thanks for that delicious dinner.
Just loved the pudding, oh so good!'
(I don't make puds – some other host).
But don't let on, although I should.
And soon he may be thanking her
for something that she didn't make,
and something that I did instead.
And will she point out his mistake?
Two dinner parties in a week
is not a marvellous recipe
for quite recalling who made what.
It can escape one's memory.
Best not to mention any food
and simply say the meal was great.
Or else you may remember later,
and feel embarrassed – and too late.

NOT THE BEST DINNER PARTY

Mary didn't click with John,
and Vic and Mike did not get on,
and Daisy really fancied Tim –
infuriating husband Jim.
And Willie banged on far too long
when telling Anna she was wrong.
And Arthur was a bloody pain.
We won't be asking him again.
What's more, the food was not that great
with too much left on every plate.
I guess we've all gone through a night
when nothing seems to work out right.

DINNER WITH THE NEIGHBOURS

We sorted out the whole of Europe,
what's more, in only two hours flat.
If only Britain's politicians
could do a little more of that.

BURNING THE CANDLE AT BOTH ENDS

Every cook, I think, has loads of candles –
half-used ones that we've never thrown away,
stuffed in plastic bags in kitchen drawers,
intended to be used another day.

None of them would last a dinner party.
Why bother with those useless candle stores?
And why complain (as I do, and quite often)
there's no space left in any of my drawers?

All those half-burned candles from last Christmas,
and probably the Christmas-time before,
and parties going back at least a decade –
a hundred there I won't use any more.

'Have a clear out!' says a voice inside me.
'Just look at all the clutter in this place!
Or don't complain again about the kitchen
and say you're always running out of space.'

POST-MORTEM

'John was a bit off tonight.'
'And Dido hardly said a word.'
'And Jim seemed pretty weird as well.'
'But not as weird as his new bird.
Gosh, what an amazing cleavage!
And how old was she, sixty plus?'
'The only thing that I much liked.'
'I thought she looked ridiculous.'

THE MORNING AFTER THE PARTY

A nicer sound than any cat –
a dishwasher that's gently purring.
A most relaxing sound is that –
a gentle purring, restful whirring.

Purring – nice when cats do that.
But nicer when dishwashers do –
reminding us of work we've saved.
I love that purring noise, don't you?

The kitchen – tidy, back to normal.
You're purring, like the washer is.
The dishwasher, a marvellous tool,
and one of life's necessities.

'BYE FOR NOW!'

'Goodbye for now! It's been a gas!'
'Ssshh, everyone! You'll wake the street!'
'Fantastic evening – thanks a lot!
And filet mignon? What a treat!'
What time is it? God, half past three.
My goodness, how the time has passed!
The hours flew by. I say goodbye,
and stagger off to bed at last.

KNOWING WHEN TO STOP

Rather a good rule in cooking
is knowing when to take a break.
Ditto a good rule in writing.
Go on too long – a big mistake.

Farewell for now to Britain's cooks,
and amateurs who, just like me,
can see the funny side of things
involved with daily cookery!

POSTSCRIPT

When my friend Cyd Barker suggested I write a book about the funny side of cooking, I was dubious at first. Were there enough humorous themes to fill a book? I could certainly write about culinary disasters, guests who'd had one too many and with dire consequences, crazy food fads and so on, and poke a bit of fun at haute cuisine and pretentious restaurants. But enough to make a book? I strongly doubted it – as other writers clearly have, since I can't think of a single humorous book on cooking, although there are plenty of recipe books written with a light-hearted touch. Nor could I recall a funny TV programme about cooking, except the 'Gourmet Evening' Fawlty Towers episode, or 'Come dine with me' which was generally more embarrassing than amusing. And the only funny films I can recall on cooking are 'Ratatouille' and 'Babe' and 'Chicken Run', which weren't really about cooking, but more about a pig and chickens escaping the cooking pot. 'Babe' put me completely off pork for ages! Apparently 'Chef' is a highly amusing film – although I haven't seen it yet.

I also questioned, in an age where so many people take cooking seriously, whether a fun book on the subject might flop as quickly as a soufflé, or fall as flat as a pancake. Nevertheless, I decided to make a few phone calls and send a few emails, and ask friends if they had any amusing stories to add to my own. The response astonished me. At least seven people recounted tales of cats and dogs scoffing meals just before the guests arrived; other quoted dinner guests behaving outrageously – falling asleep at the table or even on to the plate, or arriving on the wrong night, or even hosting a dinner party when you suddenly remember you're supposed to be at another one. Yet others were slightly more serious, bemoaning the pressure to do something new; or the frustration of supermarkets changing layouts round (especially at Christmas), and there was a reassuringly common theme for someone of my age – the conversations we can't remember at the dinner party the night before, although they seemed utterly riveting at the time.

This encouraging initial reaction suddenly poured a whole lot more thoughts into my head. Often very little things that we rarely think about. The endless mugs we have but don't need; the decanters and gadgets we never use; the partners who can't make themselves a slice of toast without us clearing away the mess and putting the lid back on the marmalade; the irritation of people on their mobiles during meals; the throwaway generation who swear by sell-by dates and will readily chuck a whole lettuce if one outside leaf is wilting (or children who will even throw out half the contents of your fridge when they come to stay). Suddenly all sorts of themes gave me food for thought – the ludicrous gadgets like banana slicers when we could easily use a knife; the endless half-candles we collect but never use; the friends who'd rather part with their husbands than their AGAs; the demise of the dining room, and so on.

Gradually I realised that the whole subject of cooking and the vast and burgeoning industry that's built up around it could be an amusing challenge; and can only hope that this book is as fun to read as it was to write. Here are all sorts of situations we've experienced – the guests from hell; the culinary flops; the friend who stays overnight and very kindly does the washing up when you've gone to bed, only to put everything back where you can't find it; and the fads and foods we either love or hate – like Marmite and beetroot.

A book for serious cooks? Probably not, even though serious cooking also has its funny side. The sheer pretentiousness of some restaurants can make me laugh. And who doesn't laugh when watching Masterchef or Bake-off? Producers know that laughter is a key ingredient of a successful show.

A recipe book this is certainly not. Our kitchen shelves are surely groaning with enough already, and if yours are anything like mine, crammed with many still-pristine books, while others are ragged and tatty, with pages splashed with sauce and olive oil. No, hopefully this book is just a recipe for a smile, 'a soufflé for light entertainment', as my publisher describes it. Most of all, my aim is to take the stuffing out of cooking and leave it in the turkey or the chicken where it should be.

True stories? Plenty! My father in law really *did* trick the famous wine writer, Cyril Ray, into thinking he was drinking Chateau D'Yquem rather than the home-made elderflower wine made from the plants in his garden. And Albert Roux really *did* have three bowls of my own home-made and chilled cucumber and mint soup and raved about it for months, even telling my husband; 'I will take the taste of it to my grave!' My one and only culinary triumph! And I really *do* have a friend who can make a food shopping trip last all day (and does), asking the shopkeepers about the origins of the food, its provenance and so on, with a vast queue of frustrated shoppers building up behind us. (Luckily she's French and doesn't speak a word of English, so won't be able to read the poem about her in this book!) And I really *do* get so into my main hobby – gardening - that I completely forget I've asked people to lunch until they're knocking at the door and I'm still in my dressing gown. And I really *have* had dinner out with a champion Ozzie surfer who ate two Porterhouse steaks in a row on our first (and last!) date.

I would like to thank my husband Donough for all his patience while I've been writing this book, and for putting up with too many salad days in the process; Prue Fox, the computer whizz who got it all together, and on whom I can bounce ideas while she gives me others, Denise Dorrance for her cover illustration; and Martin Rynja, my publisher, for his support and encouragement.